NOWHERE BETTER THAN THIS

ACKNOWLEDGEMENTS

Acknowledgements are due to the following publications in which some of these poems, or earlier versions of them, appeared: *Charlie's Mid-Life Crisis* (Right Charlie Books), *Eating Your Cake... and Having It* (Fatchance Press), *Exeter Flying Post, Headlock, The New Exeter Book of Riddles* (Enitharmon), *The North, Prop, The Rialto, Scratch, Seam, Smiths Knoll, Stride* and *Third Way.*

'His Training for the Mission Field Remembered' was commended in the 1997 Field Day/Blue Nose Poetry Competition.

'The First' was highly commended in the 1999 Jack Clemo Poetry Competition.

'Us' was inspired by a sculpture by Bill Woodrow, and was broadcast on Radio 4 in the programme *Why is a Raven Like a Writing Desk?*

'The School-Walk', 'Part-timer', 'Book Story', 'Driving to Switzerland', 'In the Brethren', "2 become 1", 'Leaving Brixton', 'What they Left Behind', 'Errand', 'Logging', 'Mustard', 'Journey', 'We are Sitting in the Blue Passat Estate', 'Parenthood', and 'The Difference' appeared in the pamphlet *The Difference* (Aldeburgh Poetry Trust, 1999).

The title is taken from a 'giveaway' art installation by the late Felix Gonzales-Torres. Thank you to Tatiana.

I am grateful to Roy Blackman, Sian Hughes, Naomi Jaffa, Michael Laskey, Mark Robinson and Peter Sansom for their comments on some of these poems in manuscript.

Cover painting by Leo McDowell courtesy of the Linda Blackstone Gallery: linda@lindablackstone.com

ANTHONY WILSON

For Bronwyn, from Anthony

NOWHERE BETTER THAN THIS

with best wishes.

worple press

First published 2002 by
Worple Press
12 Havelock Road
Tonbridge
Kent TN9 1JE

ISBN 0 9530947 8 2

Worple Press is an independent publisher specialising in poetry,
art and alternative titles. **Worple Press** can be contacted at:

12 Havelock Road, Tonbridge, Kent TN9 1JE
Email theworpleco@aol.com
Fax: 01732 352 057

Typeset and printed by Peepal Tree Press

CONTENTS

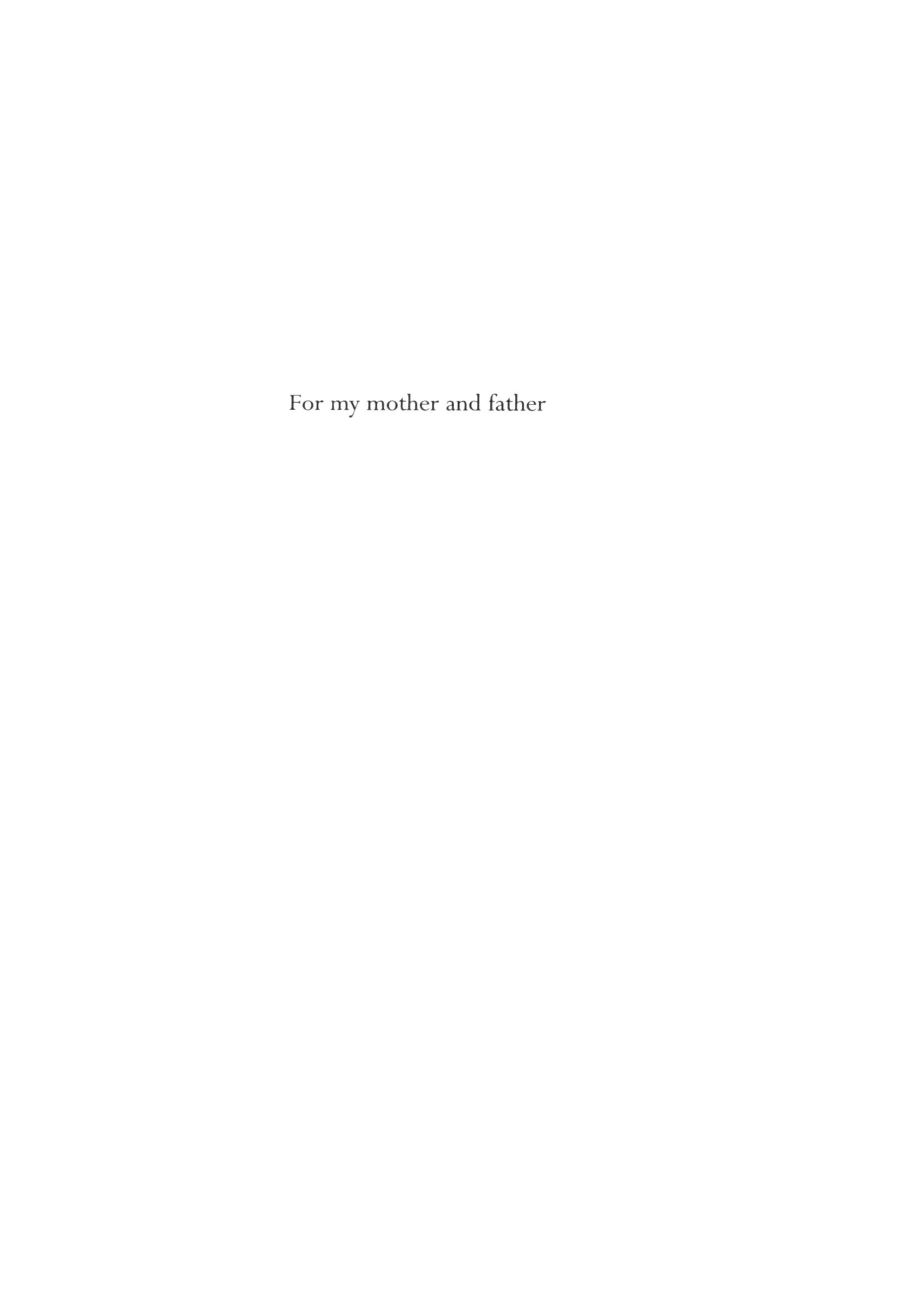

For my mother and father

Just as there is a toilet in every house,
There is a lunchbox of dung in every man

— Yorifumi Yaguchi

THIS IS ABOUT

Our Friday morning together
rediscovering how to wander
from shop to shop in search
of the perfect trousers to slob in,

the right jazz compilation to break them in to
and maybe some trainers,
the sort that have no laces,
only a pull-cord and a toggle

and which come in black,
chocolate or yeti.
This is about your hand finding mine
and in the next shop, my arm,

and pulling a shirt out for me
when it's you we're looking for,
about going on separate errands
and meeting on the second floor of the bookshop

where we choose holiday reading,
even taking time to sit cross-legged
in a corner trying out a page or two
of the new Richard Ford, Coleridge's

late life and that prize-winning teen fiction
you've had your eye on all winter.
This is about sitting upstairs
at Costas with the papers,

about me helping you with your moccachino
and also getting the shakes.
This is about the dance
of making it up as we go along,

about persuading ourselves
we could catch a film later,
or turn this into lunch at Guiseppe's,
or wander round the cathedral

then the quay for tea at Roger's
for his fabulous apple jam.
This is about catching ourselves suddenly
in changing room mirrors,

a couple from ten years ago giggling,
waving at us from the past
where they can see everything—
the children, the christenings

and the house-moves
in their self-absorbed processions—
but without the right words
of warning or love:

the kind that only come from being there,
as you drive away from the wedding party,
the first sash of pink sky in your wing mirror
daring to make you dream of happiness.

I

JOURNEY

It is dusk in Wiltshire.
Pausing for a change of guard at Westbury
I can just about make it out
on the escarpment. Not prehistoric
or Roman, nineteenth century probably,
given a new coat each May.
The suit opposite doodles next to the crossword,
the quick one, in red biro. The bar shut
for ten minutes at Reading and hasn't reopened.
With conversation more risky than poetry
I decide against asking him if I sleeptalked,
though want to, so strong was my impression
of you next to me, then above me.
In the queue behind a broken down freight
outside Bristol there's a chance to admire
who Brunel was: a genius, at twenty three,
cutting west through hillsides, rock,
woods rising sheer from the track.
With the light properly fading at Taunton
a gun dog crashes after a rabbit,
the pleased angle of a twelve bore, smoking open.
Tell me, is this what success is:
to spend more time away from home trying
to avoid the eye of the woman
with the beige T-shirt and improbable breasts,
and concentrate instead on the motorway,
now parallel with us, a herd of Friesians
inching towards the corner of a field,
a barge following its ripple
and this taxi to this door which in September
I will be putting down as expenses.

but we will not buy it.
It stinks of dogs for one thing (Labradors,
at a guess) and the spec is really poor.
Sure it's got windows, sunroof
and a boot the size of Alaska
but the miles are wrong side of 65
and for a K that's bargepole territory. Colour
isn't great, but never as bad as
that silver diesel saloon on Marsh Barton
with the hole in the carpet, one careful
chain-smoking rep, an L at only 795.
Peter's moustache spies what we don't,
though, that he's got us already: despite
our practised jargon
we can't tell brake fluid from water.
By letting us drive this crapheap
the three miles to Broadclyst
he knows we'll want something better,
that other one, terrific value, twelve hundred more
and burgundy which he'll persuade us
is 'Indian red', and rare.
By the time I write him my cheque
I don't care about full history or even
that BT owned it first: it'll get us to the Borders,
and maybe next year Lausanne
where it will stick out in the car park
to my aunt's flat as German with a Britannia Ferries
GB sticker next to its Top Marks
number plates spelt with a 'que' for a joke.

SUBSIDENCE

Dropped the car off at the garage and phoned Nick in Exeter and said
Really, if she wants to remarket I understand, and all the time I'm thinking
I really don't want to lose it, I really *don't* want to lose it,
what inordinate patience you need to hold on to politeness,
a voice that will do the business for you, remain calm, professional, neat.
Then in anger dialled my brother in Bristol and while I waited
enjoyed reliving our conversation from last night, its length,
full of in-jokes and innuendoes, confessions
made out of knowingness and half-gags,
the need to keep going coming into our voices every now and again
and defeat the silence, the miles of our lives, the years of our separation,
how he said to me after a really nice call — I'd been thanking him
for the novel he'd given me, truthfully relaying how it was just right,
how it'd made me wince with recognition, how I'd laughed, cried and felt
How does he know so much about my life? — after saying all that
(and asking the usual stuff about kids and wives and churches),
after such a nice call he asks me about the house and I tell him
It's bad, a bad survey, we have to get an engineer in
and the nearest he can do is Monday, it's basically subsidence,
we can't believe it, it never said anything about that in ours.
And then I tell him how tired we are, that Grossmama is dying in Vienna
and that's tiring too and all the time I'm thinking about the times
I used to pin him down on the floor and sit astride his chest
till he cried out 'Submit!', and how I'd punch him in the kidneys
till my hand went red, till neither of us could take any more,
and the tears that followed, my parents finding me curled in a corner
in the bathroom, sobbing 'I hit him, I hit him, I hit him'.
After the confessions, the laughter, the games of our conversation,
he pauses again to ask me What if you lose the house?
What if it's unsellable, what if you can't after all?
And I'm back in that bathroom, crying, curled up, knowing I've sinned
but wanting to start all over again hitting him till he submits.
Or that other memory I still carry and should jettison,
the one where he tells me 'What's poetry? What good does it even do?',

the voice just rising a little to show me he's not joking for once,
a tone that says I got you and you know it, and our eyes lock for a second,
he's shooting me a look that tells me he's thinking I've betrayed my ideals
of living in the city bringing healing to the oppressed and the poor.
And my mind goes to Hemingway's 'broken places'
but for some reason nothing comes out of my mouth,
I just stare at him till he turns away or makes a joke out of it (I forget).
All of this is going through me as I wait.
I am ringing him this morning to say Richard, you—,
couldn't you just have listened for once, and not asked questions,
and listened, and not asked questions, just for once?
But what I say is Grossmama's dying in Vienna, Tats is taking it badly,
you shouldn't have, what I mean is, couldn't you just have said
'I'm with you in this'?, and I know what I want to say (and still might say)
is We've got a problem on Saturday with the football,
I mean, who *do* we support? If England lose we're Swiss,
but I say none of this, I say Richard, please pray for us.

LEAVING BRIXTON

It's summer and we are living in a house
we don't own. We hang washing in the garden,
carry trays with salad and wine from the kitchen
which feels too small, and slump in front of the news

as we used to, at home, but it doesn't feel right.
The railway keeps us awake
long after we've finished worrying about
who we'll stay with next.

When your park-trip with the kids
didn't work out this morning
I kept one, you took one, and I read
to him, then fed him, then put him

down, then fed him again, his eyes closing and closing.
They looked brown. Last time they were green.
When was the last time I looked? — It's gone.
I need to be homeless more often.

WHAT THEY LEFT BEHIND

Two pallets, wooden,
one mattress, double and damp,
a police cone, a roll of carpet,
blue, threadbare and sodden,
a floodlight minus sensor,
a bucket of ashes, soot
halfway across the sitting room
floor, a chest of drawers
with THIS IS CRAP LEAVE IT
in red felt tip on a sticker,
the kitchen sink (a surprise)
and keys to the back door.

In the garden a T.V. aerial,
two iron bedsteads tangled
with bindweed, ivy,
a strimmer with a coil
of green wire, a spare key
under a stone, a toilet cistern
(with parts), a hubcap, Italian,
and a dead car battery.
In the loft twelve cardboard
boxes, one too big for the hatch,
and a lightbulb, 60 watt, the one
they forgot to take with them.

REVISING THE WELCOME PACK

I type in Wendy's number
praying they won't need it.
What I want to say
is rain will batter the window

while Radio Borders plays
'Here Comes the Sun'
to you filling hot water bottles;
that you can wake here

to heatwave, river-spate and minus 18;
that cashmere from town
allows you to contribute,
conscience-clear,

at a third of London prices;
also, that the Aga
is the oil-tanker-analogy:
taking two days to warm up

it makes entering the kitchen
after a night with the door closed
like stepping off the plane at Rhodes.
Should I say about the curry house burning down?

Or that a son was conceived here,
his sister's first steps
faltered near the fireplace,
or include the wedding guest

with Special Branch in tow
playing at waiters allowed only orange juice;
or that view of Hale Bopp
peeing on the drive

one midnight through the frost?
What you have to know
is what you can get anywhere:
Safeways is cheapest for petrol,

and foxes ransack the bins,
or a badger if you're quiet and lucky.

LOGGING

Yesterday I went logging with Jock.
Me chopping, him stacking between cigarettes.
We talked about books, about moving, our children.
He described it to me as Zen,
how if you visualise the axe splicing the log
it becomes an act of deliverance, faith even.
How the rhythm can become you over time
the desire not to lose it palpable, like sweat.
This evening I was out there on my own.
I thought how odd, a Catholic
and a Protestant divining manual labour as Zen.
Both struggling, both with boulders from childhood,
the long silence of the cup rising to the lips.
But we'd worked well together, no question.
By the time he took up the chopping
a pile was already growing, me stooping
to pick up a couple each time he paused,
and fling them flat and fast, like frisbees,
some spinning as if to fly half, breaking out of defence.
Some I didn't even watch where they landed.
There were two logs I just couldn't do.
All the Zen in the world wouldn't crack them.
Too knotted. I left them to the frost.

EARLY MORNING SWIMMERS

As I get to the pool
the serious ones,
the flat-tummied moustachioed
men with ying/yang tattoos,
the beanpole young women
in black Speedo costumes
and aquamarine swim-hats,
are just hauling themselves out,
goggles raised on their foreheads
like WWII fighter pilots
with worry-free schoolboy grins.
My group come next:
the silver-haired ladies
who gossip the entire length
of the pool; the seventy-year-
old, skin the colour of syrup,
whose unfailing breast-stroke
gets her through 30 lengths
in a half-hour; the whale-
woman, gorgeous in forget-me-
not print on white; the man
who could be my father,
pushing the water away
from his face as one might
a farmyard smell
on the patio of a holiday villa.
My favourite, though,
is the lady who swims with
her spectacles perched
on the end of her nose
as if reading the water
for a sign, or the choppy hand-
writing of an older sister retired
from teaching to Spain,
for the sun she says
in one letter, but really
for the bullfights and the men.

II

CLEANING UP THE KISS

What you spy as they continue kissing
is what we miss, invisible smuts of dust
in places we do not look. You know
every pore of them, using a fresh swab
to re-white their marble clench. Unable
to thank you as you leave the gallery they
appear to move closer, the faintest breath
of perfume brushing past them like a stranger.

USING GOOD ENGLISH

On the second day of the clear-out we find
a stack of them, enough for a class of forty,
reprinted since the fifties, their black jackets
and wraparound thin red line, like the equator,
a masterpiece of old-world understatement.

At coffee they get taken outside, and by lunch
the empty corridors and assembly hall
ring to us trying to outquote each other
with camp invocations to *think carefully*
and describe the frolics of the wind.

They have to go into the skip, we all know that,
but for weeks after small chunks appear
in the staff room, edging out the caption competition
and even the Lottery news as we struggle
to unearth its best worst paragraph.

By half term no one bothers to finish the story
which begins *Mother spread the tablecloth.*
Dad lit the primus stove. I carried the hamper.
Titty bounced around excitedly; or correct
The german was so tinny the scientist needed a microbe to see it.

We'll never find out now if father punched the burglar
in his sitting room, if there are proper adjectives
to describe the poor children from Africa,
or whatever happened to that class travelling by train
when Bloggs pulled the communication cord.

BOOK STORY

for Marian Whitehead

Two days before the Christmas vacation
and according to tradition,
he gave out the staff their books.
An annual treat, almost looked forward to
by everybody, not least for the signs
each was able to discern
in their tome of what he thought of them
exactly. Also according to tradition
each year had its own theme—
biography, gardening, the arts—
but never anything 'difficult'.
He chose with meticulous care:
a novel depicting a man grieving
his dead father went one year
to the piano teacher. To the head
of art a collection of short stories
one of which concerned a woman unable
to leave her lover for the woman
she truly loved. Comparisons were made
in the car park after dark
and from these discussions
a general consensus of unease emerged
over the volume of illustrated fairy tales
found, wrapped but unsigned
in the nursery teacher's handbag.
Not a word was said in the building.
Your narrator received a detective
fiction, French, set in the Thirties.
The translation was unspeakable.
It was said his wife worked
for the publisher, so it is likely
he obtained it without paying, I think.

THE CONVENTION WAS NEARLY OVER

After the bucket-of-water-throwing-workshop, a seminar,
'Clownery in the new Millennium: fame or money?'
He was tired, impatient to get back to his trailer
with its mirrors. First he had the conference dinner
with keynote shows from the Laughter Brothers,
Sicko the Sex Clown and Naughty Knickers Nancy.
As the emcee tapped ironically on the microphone for quiet
he knew just what the evening needed: an ice cream fight.
He'd heard how last year degenerated with the jelly,
Dave Picasso on the Pierrot table angry
with the leader of the Chaplin Group ignoring
his rescue of a drowning child.
When a spoonful disappeared down the cleavage of Elba
from the visiting *Troupe de Langue Imaginaire*
clowns dived on and under tables hurling
jelly of all colours until every costume in the dining hall shone with it.
He launched the first vanilla blob like a hand grenade then vanished
through a door labelled Fire Escape. He knew in the long run
he was doing them all a huge favour.

NOVEL

He decided to make things better:
start swimming at lunchtime,
cycle into town, cut down
on the booze, try not to shout at the kids,
do the school run for a neighbour,
help, maybe even start a diary,
maybe even that novel, the one about
a man with no car and no money,
in a strange city, having just walked out
on his job, his family, his lover,
who takes up swimming and cycling
whose sole diary entry each autumn tells
about leaves, how he'd time now to kick them,
not like before, in the hard days,
when he began talking to himself,
when he crashed the car, when he slept
in the garden, when he grew a beard
and his hair so he could visit
when the mood took him and watch them
being picked up or playing in the park,
who was that woman, she seemed to know
everyone by sight, if not by name.

THE LETTER

We are halfway through the gate
before we realise he is not coming.

I leave her in the rain and run back in
to fetch him, face six inches from *Zoo Lane.*

He falls completely stiff so I drag him
across the boards while he screams I hate you.

This is when the doorbell shrills,
the postman with a letter with insufficient postage.

I lost the baby, it says,
before I could name him after you.

MY FOX

after Raymond Carver

A fox came into my garden.
Not Aesop's, or Chaucer's,
or the fox of William Shakespeare.
Nor Ben Jonson's, nor that of Dr Seuss.
It was unlike most foxes that you see
in that it looked like a fox.

It was not Ted Hughes' fox
who had made plans to go fishing that day
but found himself instead on the point
of being torn to shreds by a pack of baying hounds;
it was not Philip Larkin's fox:
the view of a cemetery at 3 o'clock in the morning
in the rain
disguised as a fox;
it was not Seamus Heaney's fox
which had lain buried for centuries
under a pub in West Belfast
and so knew a thing or two about life as a fox,
so well preserved were his faculties;
nor was this laughing Sam Beckett's fox
who had no arms and no legs and no tail
and who lived in a dustbin on a dungheap
playing chess with its snout
against no-one
but who was reputedly one of the most cheery foxes the sun ever
blessed
with its rays;
nor was it that nice Ezra Pound's fox,
created in part from the bones of other foxes
and whom fox-hunters everywhere respected
but never really as it were admitted to *liking;*
nor was it T.S. Eliot's fox

in the garden
the garden
the garden before dawn
the eternal dawn before time
when History is Now and the Fox;
and it was not Wallace Stevens' fox
which was really thirteen different foxes
each of them nothing to do with being a fox;
it was not the fox in translation,
a cunning ruse of a metaphor
smuggling dissent into the minds of the proletariat
against state control over aspects of daily life such as
chicken coops, wire fencing and hunting laws;
nor was it even Raymond Carver's fox
which did its best to act like a regular fox
but had in fact just left his wife
and developed a drink problem:

no. It was none of these foxes.
It was a fox. I mean — it was a fox.
It stood still for a second, listening, in my garden.
It had a scar on its left flank.
Then it walked, like a fox walks, silently out of my life.

ON LUST

I have been reading Q's thesis in the library
and what a load of old rubbish it is.

Did Bordieu change nappies? —
I think we should be told.

Outside, the tennis court having it first haircut,
the groundsman bent feudally at his shadow.

Bourgeois? But of course:
last night we sat on the floor

eating meatballs with penne
in front of the Simpsons,

what I call family life.
Before thrashing them to sleep

I kiss them, obviously, twice,
my mother taught me everything.

The semiotics section is the only place,
all the best labels, plus the giggling sweet-eaters.

Was Eliot right about breasts?
I think he was. (I think he was.)

SKINNY

The day Paterson held magnesium
in the Bunsen without tongs
and got himself whisked to hospital
with second degree burns
eight years before they invented
Flamazine in the Falklands

was the day I knew one day I'd die,
my faith in God less tested
than my love of *The White Album* he'd lent me,
'Revolution 9' spinning round my head
as I turned to see him stretching
to ignite the starburst of flame.

Us

Everything opaque about us, perhaps
that's why they fill us with holes
and hang our heads for trophies —
to cut us down to size.

Down: where our number is heading
and what you can't get from us —
us with our ironing board skin,
ears like the maps of continents,

the car-tyre screech of our cries.

FOR AFTERWARDS

I want it kept simple.
I want to leave one part of the congregation
thinking they have witnessed a jazz improvisation,

another that they have attended a poetry reading
and yet another that a sermon wasn't preached at all —
the kind I long to hear still,

including a story about a boy building a toy boat,
a mention of the Prodigal Son,
a metaphor concerning train drivers,

and finally a line, tantalising and incomplete,
from one of the minor prophets
about weeping and coming home.

Someone from the world of third eleven cricket should speak,
as should the lady from the greengrocer's
who knows me as an expert on the weather and child-rearing.

I leave you with no chiselled *bon mot* from the other side.
I direct you instead to the cracker-jokes
in the suit you will bury me in,

the postcard I keep in the middle drawer
of my desk, blank but for the line:
'This green notebook is a good time in my life.'

THE SMALL PROVINCIAL CITY OPEN MIC POETRY THING

for Ann Gray and Alan Peacock

Is it the woman who begins
It's that vegetable time of year again,
her husband taking the part of the seed;

the leather-jacketed comedian
who sings in his tribute to Leonard Cohen
my hopeless persona/fell hopelessly over?

At half time we hide in our cliques:
the regulars in a large group on the sofas,
huddling together for warmth

but determined not to offer praise
of another's two minutes' glory;
the semi-pro with friends from the real world

and the guest poet and organiser
swivelling heads for contact beyond
the last-minute pleadings

of the gent in the lilac fedora
and Dr Who scarf clutching his life's work
in three foolscap folders.

In whatever season we leave it is raining,
the dream of doing more, not better, next time,
spurring us back to our talent and our rooms.

III

DRIVING TO SWITZERLAND

The night before, my father would lay out
on his side of the bed: wallet, camera, maps,
francs, washbag and passports,
meticulous as an assassin. Downstairs
my mother hissed at the kitchen floor.

At five the next morning her hand wobbled on your shoulder
and we sleepwalked through clothes to the car.
Breakfast was cornflakes on the beach at Dover,
and grit in marmalade sandwiches.
And there'd be a photograph. Nobody spoke.

On the ferry you could want to die.
We'd huddle on deck with thermos and anoraks
while my father unfurled a map deploying us
like tentpegs in a groundsheet.
We churned an unrelenting wake of Englishness.

France was always *too hot* and lunch was horseflies
and sunburn. Once we parked next to the Metro.
Speaking through my mother at the gendarmerie
my father didn't flinch when he listed as the contents
of his suitcase *twelve ties.* It was the maps he missed.

You woke next morning to scooters in alley ways
and women in slippers and dressing gowns staggering
under baguettes. Coffee. A man cursing his car.
(This could be Dijon, Lyons or Besançon.)
We slept badly because the pillows were *like rocks.*

Then that last leg through Pontarlier and the hills.
The highest big town in Europe, boys, the clouds
like a lake in the valley. Finally a door opened
and a new accent would start. My mother ceased translating.
The welcome we had walked into flew straight over our heads.

MUSTARD

Whenever you fly over
we ask you to bring mustard,
'Dijon — only 90p — *incredible.'*

We eat it with sausage casserole,
once a week in the winter,
and you know it makes

a perfect vinaigrette, quite fiery.
You frown as I shake in
the Aromat.

Once, after presenting us the jar,
you blurted 'It was the last thing
I thought would happen.

I wasn't looking for it
and definitely neither was she.'
At the end

a knife stabs up the jar's walls
as though searching for daylight.
We never get all of it out.

We wash the jar afterwards
but rarely recycle it.
It goes out with the other rubbish.

THE WALLET MY GRANDFATHER GAVE ME

is in use again. For ten years
it's rested in my desk drawer,
put into retirement by the one you bought me on Skiathos.
We lay on the roof and undressed each other.

I was hearing voices in those days,
would have gone mad without you.
Goat bells in the mists of the olive groves.
The first time I ever swam naked.

The day it went into the drawer
I pulled out of it your photograph
and a ticket to a place called Hildenborough,
cardboard, stiff, a single.

IN THE BRETHREN

Dad, what am I doing here?
What is it I am doing now?
Are you proud of me?
—W.S. Graham

The cough-thick silence
put everyone in their place.

We were told:
If you speak, make sure you speak to God.

If you were a child you could not speak.
If you were a lady you could not speak.

When I first spoke I heard
my voice say '— and Jesus still loved

Peter. He took him in his arms
and forgave him as a father would his

son.' Outside your hand tensed on my shoulder.
'You showed great insight in there.

Well done.' I stood there
renewed and released, your hoped-for

unimagined blessing
shocking

me into places
where church could not go. Let differences

be differences.
Likenesses, likenesses. Wrap me up in your arms.

ANOTHER CALL TO RICHARD

This time late at night about Andrew,
whom we'd baby-sit on fine June evenings in the suburbs.
What about Andrew, I say. Are you going?
You've got to haven't you, he says.
I mean we knew him. Only 27, I say.
He was all right, really, Andrew, he says,
I mean, I liked him. I liked him too, I say.
Are you going, he says. I suppose, I say.
I mean, I should, I want to, I liked him too.
I say it again. I liked him too.
What do you remember? he says.
I remember, I say,
I remember his smile, he says,
you know, confident, but shy.
His smile, I say, I remember that.
I remember him asking you about school,
you know, the questions pouring, on and on at you.
And he punched me once in the balls,
must have been about seven,
didn't mean to, he just was the wrong height.
Twenty seven, he says, twenty seven.
He was never Andy, though, was he, I say, always Andrew.
Yes, he says, it's funny.
He never went to bed, did he.
He never went to bed, he says.
All those questions, about everything, he never stopped.

THE FIRST

It begins on Christmas Eve, when, after an early night
you can't sleep, like childhood, your room strange with new
furniture, the pull-cord by your headboard long gone.
One of your children is coughing. You rise and after promising
milk, glimpse the garden greying with frost, pause
to mist the window with a sigh, unlock the kitchen door
and stare into the fridge the way you used to after
the last tube, when all you heard was the wind
in the silver birch they planted on your first,
a reminder, upright, brown only once in that drought,
that you were theirs and however far you travelled
they would always be here.
How true that is
and whether you care you'll find out in five hours
on their bed with the stockings, careful not to thank them
directly. She used to take care of those too
but that's not what you miss. When he drags you out
for golf and she builds you a fry-up afterwards you notice
all that hasn't changed is the station and the bookshop
where you swore you wouldn't leave and read her
the *Rubaiyat* to prove it. Like the sudden rain
on his windscreen, it comes back what she wanted
to go out to '—Louis Armstrong, not the Beatles. *Think*.
If you can't remember a thing I say, why don't you make a list?'

MEMBURY

Was the hour-mark from home,
its guy-roped radio mast visible five minutes away,
on winter nights an eye-sized ember blinking at its tip.

Membury, where the wind off the plain is a knife,
petrol-outpost for the desperate, coffee-refuge
for men sitting singly outstared by their reflections;

where we never stopped, not even to pee or for gum,
place-between, time-point, neither family nor school,
our conversation eddying as your wedding ring

tapped Telemann on the steering wheel,
the miles charging by in a blur of furrows and sheep.
Did you know where you were driving us?

— Not only to masters who taught you,
the ancient hunger and cold, but cigarettes fumbled
in bushes, madness and stealing towels,

boys being kicked downstairs, kicked for crying,
kicked to stop them phoning home?
None of us kept a diary.

On clear nights at Membury we gazed into that
and said nothing. I can see you refuelling
with apple pie on the way back, toying, as you pull out,

with picking up that hitcher who reminds you
of your son. If I was that hitcher now I'd ask
Take me back to Membury. Buy me a coffee and we'll talk.

WEDDING DAY

A pair of black shoes in the hall,
and my father speaking softly about loss.

After the most careful shave of my life
it is my mother counting in French

the placements for a meal I won't eat
while my uncle chooses a suit

from my brother's empty wardrobe.
The thousands I kissed, and never kissed.

I will leave my speech in the greenhouse...
so from now on it's going to be ad lib, all of it.

1974

Our tennis whites shine.
There is the crunch of gravel
as the green gate clicks.
A milk float wafts by.

One elderly mixed doubles
wave and smile without speaking.
At the last court we come to
the holes in the netting are boy-sized.

After twelve deuces a backhand goes in,
the one game he allows me.
You were lucky to get that one
he says, leading me up the steps by the ivy.

I AM BECOMING MY DAD

The way I let coffee grow cold,
build skyscrapers of bills on my desk,
and will look at a map only once,
especially when lost. I catch him
in my *Well done* to their pictures
and needing to beat them at Memory.

Never knowingly wrong,
I'll argue the semantics of 'going to'
for an hour. Like him, I buy
only one brand of red, am faithful
to the same pair of brogues,
resoling them before weddings.

Twins in edginess during rugby
we love Bond films, keep cheque book
stubs, would kill for a fry-up.
My sister says I've inherited
his trouble with piles. Unlike him,
I can't tell if she's serious.

HELP

A chill day in the garden with the kids.
Do you want me to go on?

Me neither, but I think we all know by now
I'm not here to help you.

They made mudpies and I weeded.
Dug. Weeded. Whatever.

Are they the same?—
ask my brambles.

On my List Of Things To Do is the lawn
and so is starting a list.

Will I always be like this?
Of course, it's your father, says my mother

as if *that* explains everything.
How marvellous to be told you are useless

in a study overlooking the rose garden.
(I made that last bit up.)

Already they know about green fingers
and tiny seeds growing *bigger as the sky.*

That's not to say they won't mess up
like I have:

we chose their godparents well.
If I kept the best wine till last

it was an accident.
If I do sound tired, I am.

PART-TIMER

He gets here always on time —just —
wearing a smile not a sack like the rest of us.

We find him reading books in the library
and, worse, writing.   Seriously,

how can we take him? Those educated vowels
and that stoop; that ever-so-careful

pause holding doors. Doesn't do playground,
doesn't stay for meetings, doesn't know he's born.

Ask him to show you his file and all you get
is a grin. Try him for lesson plans: he forgets.

Won't come to the pub and can't be arsed with lunch.
Says like he totally means it we're a *great bunch*

to work with. Is it us or is he taking the piss?
No, nowhere else. You've got me all to yourselves.

THE LESSON

When we get to the bunkers
we imagine a fried egg,
the ball a yolk I am lifting out
leaving the white intact.

My swing is natural
but my grip is all wrong.
I tee up my headmaster's eyeball
and slice him off the planet.

TWO HALVES

for Rupert Loydell

We enter the pub and I flick the switch
from New-Man-Dad to Chelsea fan.
In the other bar they've Sky on a giant
screen. We're two-nil down to Leeds, away. The pitch
looks terrible. You chuckle into your Heineken.

OK, so I'm not the man you thought I was.
But I need this half hour of mindless escape
just as much as you need that pint.
Mine's a half, if that's all right. Yes, it's because
of the time. And yes, I do know they're crap.

It's got nothing to do with logic and everything
with being seven in the last year they won something.
You either understand that or you don't.
I pity you because you just can't see it. Or won't.

THE PRELIMINARIES

I love the preliminaries at internationals,
the camera panning down the ranks of players,
arms locked behind them, bringing every follicle,
every pore to us, their nervousness,

the flat unashamed cry of their singing
ahead of the band and the crowd,
vaseline glowing on their foreheads,
gumshields flashing, their hard swallowing

faces shivering, thighs jerking
their knees forward, the glazed
handshakes with royalty sending
them trotting off like schoolboys

to face the opening whistle, crowd-bay,
wind-tears, the thunder.

'2 BECOME 1'

In the newly-opened Virgin
there's a video playing *Lady*
and the Tramp, silently, incongruous
with *This is Hardcore:* we join
it at the moment when the Tramp
leads the dog-catcher a merry
dance over and back a three
foot fence, the chase leading him
as we know to 'Snob Hill' or, as the Bulldog
with the 'gor-blimey accent has it
later 'Miss Park Avenue 'erself.'
You know by now this is my way
of saying sorry for having no money,
by spending money on something
we don't need and are only 60%
certain we like. 'I don't know
what it's called,' I stumble, before
delivering it, note-perfect, to the smiling
assistant and queue of one goth and two
truanting nine-year olds, red
with embarrassment: 'It's for a friend.'

BREAKFAST WITH CHARLIE PARKER

After feeding the goldfish,
he eats three bowls of Shreddies
and a slice of peanut butter toast
washed down with tea from his
favourite Chelsea mug, plus
a glass of long-life orange juice.

He chatters nineteen to the dozen
about guns and Halloween,
charges out to watch television.
During *Rugrats* the notes begin
their journey round the house
and London really burns.

LEONARD COHEN IS MY BARBER

He works at Tony's, Northcote Road,
three doors down from the bookshop,
backwater of antiques and health food.

He isn't the owner, though could be,
if he wanted, preferring to hover at No.3,
'the quiet one' in the corner by the door,

his conversation elegant and clipped,
never far from remembrance or prayer.
We nod at each other like accomplices

and he beckons me to my chair.
He vanishes a second from the mirror
adorned with *Babes of New York*

and *Five Views of Cyprus* postcards
as he flicks the cape out in front of me.
His fingers tuck in the tissue,

their whiff of Marlborough and aftershave
knowing what I want already —
No. 2 round the sides and back

and the best he can do with the top.
I want to ask about Marianne,
Janice and Kris, about unmade beds,

raincoats and dockyards.
I catch him from the corner
of my eye avoiding me,

his lips pursed with regret.
'Do you mind they all say you're miserable,
a byword for cod-depression?'

Showing me the back of my head
his fingers tremble on the hand-mirror,
his mouth open slightly as if caught

in revelation, the radio busy now
with The Carpenters,
and rain mysteriously clearing,

like fog lifting from a harbour
or a woman's back, her dress
sliding without hurry to the floor.

POST-OP

Happy because I am here, not there,
opposite Frank Tyson's namesake recounting
demob from the RAF, getting bowling hints
in a ward the former guest wing of a duke;
South African Ingrid who called me dear, darling,
brought me Marmite when I asked for honey
and touched my arm; Jane from 'Nin-Zid',
Mr Wilson to her, sorry to always get to me last;
and Monica who said she'd look out for my book;
to have escaped smiling, woken up on morphine,
tried some passable pork casserole whose fault it wasn't
I vomited and more Radio 4, half asleep,
than I remember — though when you ask me news
out it all comes verbatim: a journalist shot dead
in Tyrone, the same, only captured without a passport
on the Afghan border, and more reaction to Berlusconi:
how the world outside goes on, like after birth,
without knowing how drole I was going under.

HIS TRAINING FOR THE MISSION FIELD REMEMBERED

We were all crazy or stupid.
Some of us got out alive, many escaped
only with their addictions.

Those in the female population
were lucky if they left
without being stabbed.

The Masters were all drunkards or saints.
Or queer.
Chapel was four times daily.

We warmed the older boys' beds
by lying in them, naked,
and farting.

Beatings were frequent and public.
One boy drowned himself in the swimming pool in December.
The water was black and full of leaves.

Sport was a frozen leather ball with razors.
In summer there were dunkings in the brook
though — unofficially — they took place all year round.

Those who survived rarely speak,
even in letters.
By 'female population' I mean girls.

HE DIDN'T KNOW WHAT TO DO WITH IT

so he put it in the bin.
But if I leave it there
things could get sticky.
He carried it outside
and started to dig a hole.
Up to his waist in earth
he changed his mind again:
he'd heard stories of things like this
getting into the water table.
He looked at his watch.
An hour before they got home.
So why he found himself driving past the dump,
out of town, towards the fields,
he had no clue.
He took the second turn off the trunk road
and the third turn off the track off that.
He stopped at the first farm he came to
and went up to the door.
When no-one answered he knew he was home.
He was just lifting it out of the boot
when a voice exploded across the farmyard.
He had no option but to stick the farmer
in the container as well,
only with all the liquid, he wouldn't fit,
unless he could lose the legs.
It was becoming a problem.

I AM TO BLAME

for your eczema, but not, for once,
for money. Supper, that disaster, ok, yes.
But not the iron packing up
nor the washing machine man showing
three hours late requiring tea and the last
digestive. Of course I left a note on the door
while I picked them up. So he did
another job in the meantime,
so what? In Pinhoe, I grant you,
but that's enterprise culture and that is not
my fault. The sheets are nearly dry now
by the way — we could make the bed, then test
whether it was them made you itch like this.

LATE AUGUST FRAGMENT

Autumn but not autumn, summer
but not. Tomorrow is a new sunrise

but for now I watch the struggle
of four beautiful Kenyans

round the 3,000m steeplechase in Seville,
one of whom will become immortal

before the night is through.
Yesterday, when everything seemed possible,

I cut myself shaving, and bled a little.
'I have no confidence in these matters

but am willing to pursue the dream,'
Cassirer doesn't say, and I agree.

Downstairs the etc etc and ER
being moving without me.

I am missing it just to be with *you.*
Who've I listened to recently? Fears,

certainly, the impossible bumblebee of truth
circling and circling me like death.

I am writing this to stay alive, by the way,
not the other way round.

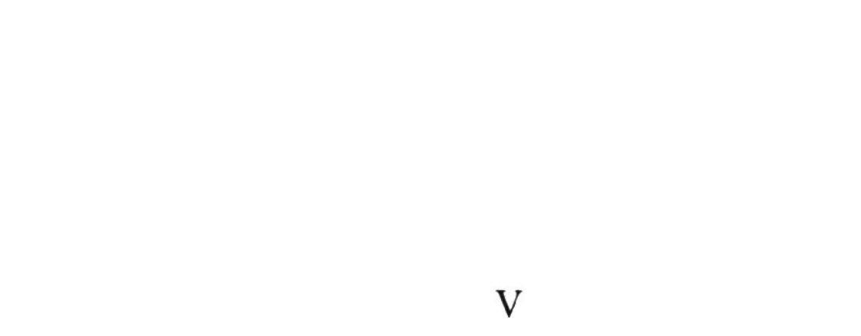

V

PARENTHOOD

after Theodore Roethke

I have known the inexorable sadness of children's shoes,
squat in their boxes, scuffed after five minutes' wearing,
the incalculable tristesse of Thomas the Tank Engine slippers,
dayglo blue nylon with immutable plastic badges,
and the cost of all this which is sleeplessness, vomit and Dettox spray,
rage of shoelace tying,
bottom wiping, yoghurt scraping, Ribena mopping,
as you try, one hand glued to your hair, your mouth burning
with sores, to speak politely on the telephone
to the woman who is buying your house,
the doctor who says don't bend, the friend who is just back from Prague,
your mother who begins 'Well, in my day...'.
And I have seen dust collect under their beds, there is nothing
I can do to prevent it, visions of gin, gallons of it, before breakfast,
incomprehensible gobbledegook of Tommee Tippee instructions,
Tixylyx, dawn-light of Calpol, poignancy of vests in their packets,
blockage of buggies in swing-doors
and heartbreak of stories by the fire,
Granpa, Peepo!, Peace at Last, the firelight wavering
and breathing slowing to a pulse
that overcomes you with drowsiness,
the furies of your life ebbing as the story, here, now, unfurls,
grows, is fixed, not a word omitted or changed,
by stories are we known and do tell ourselves, Daddy,
I'm tired now please, carry me, you forgot vitamins, to bed.

HIS FIRST WEEK

Which was half a week, really —
he still hasn't stayed for lunch —
'Can't I go back, do I have to again?'
He has a buddy
'Which isn't a friend, it's a big boy.'
When he pees he uses the Rhine.
Trigger, the school cat, has appeared,
but he hasn't stroked him yet.
He has done painting, play-dough and bricks
but says he can't remember a thing.
In these last afternoons together
we cycle into town and visit shops
with escalators. Usually there's a bun.
I challenge him at snakes and ladders
and snail's pace racing, honours about even.

CHANGING HIM ASLEEP

after Sharon Olds

Those nights when sleep is a rope ladder you hang from,
arms above your head like handlebars,
fists clenched tight, your breath like waves
on shingle, are my favourite;
when I know I can roll you over —
and though your hands will startle an instant like starfish,
or one eye might open to interrogate me
with its indifference for a second —
that you will remain airborne, unconscious.
I go back to that first time,
two days out from hospital, alone with you at last:
the amazing transparent arc of your spray,
whilst you dreamt, soaking my legs;
and my laughter, half disbelief,
half shock, shouting into the doorway
your mother had just vacated
I don't believe it, come and look what he's done, thinking
Is this it? Yes, this is it.

ERRAND

Behind, my children, my life.
The bakery is open.

A man is laying crates of bread,
one on top of the other,
in the boot of a waiting car.

The newspaper boy wobbles on his bike.

Walking back, I tuck the loaf
under my arm, my hand cupped
round it. At school we carried
rugby balls the same way.

It left the other hand free
for punching friends and enemies
as they sauntered past.

FEBRUARY

It is not cold.
And isn't this freedom,
to sit here on a Sunday
having got up at six,
dosed him with milk,
made tea, flicked through
yesterday's *Independent*
and now to be plucking
black grapes from a white
bowl, listening to the fridge
shiver and settle and reminding
myself that hum is the fan-
oven defrosting chicken
breasts which later I will
cook in the traditional
manner with the radio,
garlic and bacon. I did
so want today to be happy.

WAKING WITHOUT YOU

I pay more attention to the news:
Ted Heath's last speech in the Commons,
the weather not saying *Southwest.*
Seeing you off at five means breakfast
feels like lunch.
                    The first time you vanished
in a storm I found them curled into you
in the guest-bed, then tiptoed out, washed,
breakfasted alone and nearly felt
like a bachelor again ducking
into the car through my aftershave.

MY BOY'S HANDS

At night they twirl your hair to sleep.
When the washing machine
comes into land they clutch your ears
at the invasion. They spot islands
in old plasticine and twist a yard
of sellotape round a loo-roll torch.

I TRY NOT TO SHOUT AT THEM

but I do: breakfast, bedtimes,
after a glass of Chardonnay —
I am not fussy. They run off
laughing, pretending not to be hurt,
then I shout some more.

Stepping on Lego is a good one,
so is spilt apple juice. During *Cold Feet*
they do not even get eye contact.
In the morning I say *No you can't*
use my lip-salve, you'll only break it.

FIRST THING

for Michael Laskey

Shunting back my bowl,
I try out among the cereals
the first thing to enter my head;

the hour I bathe in peach bubbles,
before phone, fax, and email
pull on the hem of my sweater;

the hour of blackbirds and milkmen,
of parcels, muffled
behind the door-curtain, pre-radio.

Sometimes I merely remember my name,
practising my luck like piano scales,
looking forward to it like tea.

THE TIMES

05:00 hours is bad and anything with a three in it,
for example 03:13. Those times between 02:00 and 04:00
are crippling for the next day's decisions as are those times
on a Sunday and most times during the ravages of February.
Unspeakable times include 04:59 and 01:07 — but for some reason
05:58 is not a bad time, unlike its cousins 01:58 and 02:58
who are total buggers and always will be. Among the joke-times
are anything before midnight, the lucid moments just after midnight
and those just after making love, with sleep approaching.

The why-even-bother-times are as follows: 06:14, 06:27, 06:32
and the infrequently-mentioned 06:02. The I-want to-die-now-times
list 02:09, 04:11 and 03:33. The fact we all go on living regardless
must point to something, the resilience of the human spirit, perhaps,
equality of opportunity for fathers, or even Japanese alarm clock reliability.
However, my familiarity with 04:19 of late has wrenched the bottom
drawer from my desk and scattered the contents blowing across the park
to be laughed at by children and dogs. I find this is inducing in me
a quite serious indifference to most subjects, even my work.

THE DIFFERENCE

for Jim

The lives we're living,
what difference do they make?

We wake up,
throw our children in the air
and catch them laughing
into our arms.

Friends come and go, seasons pass,
the leaves collect silently
in the garden.

Which reminds me,
there's pruning to be done
and bonfires to build.

What is it that we're doing
in this world to make it better,
a place more easy to wake in
for our children?

In the middle of all this
I am amazed
the sun still finds time
to rise beautifully over these roofs
and never asks anything in return.

THE SCHOOL-WALK

They hop down the path, pausing
to kick crab-apples, but terrified
of stepping on one. Then out through
the gate and before it clacks shut
they're off on the ten-second, headlong
sprint down the hill, till they collapse,
gasping theatrically on the low wall
by the language-school steps. Instead
of cajoling them up (it took me
two terms to learn this) I march past
to wait at the corner where no one
indicates left, seventy yards from home,
easily our most dangerous moment.
Then Dog Poo Alley, their favourite,
clean the last few weeks, almost disappointing;
past Jon-the-curate's house; over the cul-de-sac
where Liz has just moved in,
next door to the Labour-voting
skin specialist Mandy says is selling up
because he has too much space. We pick
our way through the traffic and the rest is straight.
The Royal Deaf School playing field tries to shine
in the morning's first attempt at sun
as Merenna sings 'Straw Belly Fields'
at top volume making the lollipop lady smile
an instant, the traffic parted like an ocean
and us still looking forward to the other side.

Worple Press is an independent publishing house that specialises in poetry, art and alternative titles. *Worple Press* can be contacted at:
12 Havelock Road, Tonbridge, Kent TN9 1JE Tel 01732 367 466
Fax 01732 352 057 email: theworpleco@aol.com.
Trade orders: Central Books Tel 020 8986 4854

Titles Include:

***Sailing to Hokkaido* – Joseph Woods**
(A5 Price £6.00 ISBN 0 9530947-6-6, pp. 60)
Winner of the Patrick Kavanagh Award for Best First Collection

'If Woods is technically expert it is not to dazzle but to reveal his subject matter... his work as a whole shows an impressive reach and range'

Eiléan Ní Chuilleanáin

***The Falls* – Clive Wilmer**
(A5 Price £6.00 ISBN 0 9530947-3-1, pp. 48)

'An utterly English faith in the language's passionate reticence'

Ruth Padel

'Boldly lyrical, broad in reference, felicitous in the craft of verse'

Elizabeth Jennings

***Choosing an England* – Peter Carpenter**
(A5 Price £5.95 ISBN 0 9530947-0-7, pp. 48)

'Honest, considered and moving... Peter Carpenter has tied some new marriage knot around post-modernist and mainstream verse...'

David Morley

***A Ruskin Alphabet* - Kevin Jackson**
(A6 Price £4.50 ISBN 0 9530947-2-3, pp. 88)

'If you have not yet had enough Ruskin, you may like to consult *A Ruskin Alphabet* by Kevin Jackson, a collection of facts about and opinions on

Ruskin and Ruskinites, together with a variety of pithy remarks from the man himself...'

Jim Campbell TLS

***Looking In All Directions* – Peter Kane Dufault**
(A5 Price £10.00 ISBN 0 9530947-5-8, pp. 188)

'He observes the physical world keenly, and idiosyncratically, and frequently serves the "didactic muse", but he can sing from the heart too. Even at his most personal he is reaching for something fundamental about the relationship between man and nature. It is surprising that other publishers have ignored Dufault; but Worple Press have done him proud'

John Greening TLS

'Wonderful stuff'

Ted Hughes

***Of Science* – David Morley & Andy Brown**
(A5 Price £6.00 ISBN 0 9530947-4-X, pp. 48)

A sample of poems by contemporary poets who are also trained as scientists. The mode of selection is modelled on the 1802 Lyrical Ballads, in the spirit of Miroslav Holub's notion of 'serious play', with the shared belief of Wordsworth and Coleridge that *'poetry is the breath and finer spirit of all knowledge; it is the impassioned expression which is the countenance of all science'*.

***The Great Friend and Other Translated Poems* – Peter Robinson**
(A5 Price £8.00 ISBN 0 9530947-7-4, pp. 75)

This collection brings together a choice of Peter Robinson's translations from the last quarter of a century. These are translations that remain faithful to their originals while, thanks to the poet's imaginative identifications and technical expertise, becoming English poems in their own right. The book chronicles a commitment to twentieth-century Italian poetry and to the work of Pierre Reverdy, Noriko Ibaragi and Ingeborg Bachmann.